George F.

Miniatures and borders from the Book of hours of Bona Sforza, Duchess of Milan

George F.

Miniatures and borders from the Book of hours of Bona Sforza, Duchess of Milan

ISBN/EAN: 9783742834447

Manufactured in Europe, USA, Canada, Australia, Japa

Cover: Foto ©Thomas Meinert / pixelio.de

Manufactured and distributed by brebook publishing software
(www.brebook.com)

George F.

Miniatures and borders from the Book of hours of Bona Sforza, Duchess of Milan

MINIATURES AND BORDERS

FROM

THE BOOK OF HOURS

OF

BONA SFORZA, DUCHESS OF MILAN

IN THE

BRITISH MUSEUM

WITH INTRODUCTION BY

GEORGE F. WARNER, M.A.

ASSISTANT KEEPER OF MANUSCRIPTS

PUBLISHED BY THE TRUSTEES

1894

NOTICE.

———

THE reproductions in this volume represent the choicest miniatures and borders in the exquisitely illuminated Book of Hours of Bona Sforza, Duchess of Milan, which the late Mr. John Malcolm, of Poltalloch, so generously presented to the Trustees of the British Museum in 1893 ; supplemented by a border from the "Sforziada" in the Grenville Library, which has been added for purposes of comparison.

No more perfectly finished illuminated manuscript than the Sforza Book of Hours could have been chosen for the purpose of exemplifying the best work of the miniaturists of the Milanese and Flemish Schools of the close of the fifteenth and beginning of the sixteenth centuries ; and, although the colouring of the originals is wanting in the reproductions, the fine details of the drawing and the artistic merits of the composition will not fail to excite the admiration of the student of art.

The plates, in permanent collotype, have been skilfully executed by the Autotype Company ; and the work has been superintended, and the Introduction has been written, by my colleague, Mr. G. F. Warner, the Assistant Keeper of this Department.

EDWARD J. L. SCOTT,
Keeper of Manuscripts.

DEPARTMENT OF MSS.,
6th September, 1894.

INTRODUCTION.

HE beautifully illuminated manuscript known as the "Sforza Book of Hours" was brought to this country in 1871 by Sir J. C. Robinson, who had purchased it shortly before at Madrid. The Treasury having refused to provide the means for its acquisition by the State, it passed into the hands of a more appreciative private collector, the late Mr. John Malcolm, of Poltalloch. It is due to his public spirit that the loss to the nation proved after all only temporary. In 1893, with rare munificence, he presented the volume to the British Museum, which thus adds to its treasures one of the very finest extant examples of Italian renaissance art as applied to the decoration of service-books and other manuscripts.

The MS., which is numbered Additional 34,294, is of small size, measuring only 5¼ inches in height by 4 inches in width. In its present state it consists of 348 leaves of fine vellum, and is enriched with no less than 64 full-page miniatures, besides as many as 139 equally attractive illuminated borders. When it arrived in England it formed a single volume only, in covers of faded red velvet with silver clasps. This binding, however, was of no older date than the latter part of the 17th century, and, as many of the leaves wanted guarding, Mr. Malcolm had the book newly bound in four parts. The text, all in Latin, is as follows:—(1) Cursus Evangelii, comprising short extracts from the four Gospels, f. 1 ; (2) Hours of the Holy Cross, f. 13 ; (3) Hours of the Holy Spirit, f. 28 ; (4) Hours of the Blessed Virgin, f. 41 ; (5) Lessons of the Passion, viz. Luke xxii. 1 to xxiii. 53, f. 137 ; (6) Prayers to our Lord on the Passion, f. 167 b ; (7) Prayers to the Virgin, f. 169 *b* ; (8) Memorials of Saints, each consisting of a short prayer on a single page, with a miniature, f. 186 ; (9) Seven Penitential Psalms, f. 213 ; (10) Litany, etc., f. 236 ; (11) Office of the Dead, f. 258 ; (12) "Oratió de Nomine Iesu ex Paulinis Epistolis congesta," ff. 343–348. With the exception of the last, which is an addition of no interest apparently written about the year 1600, these divisions constitute an ordinary Book of Hours, all that calls for remark being the absence of the usual calendar. At the same time, although the text as it stands is complete, many of the leaves in various places did not belong to the original MS., but fill lacunæ unhappily caused by its mutilation. As will be shown presently, these later leaves were inserted between 1519 and 1521. Altogether, they make up a third of the whole bulk, and among them are included sixteen of the miniatures, which, besides being thus of a more recent date than the rest, are of a widely different school.

To some extent the MS. tells its own history. From the text, indeed, we only learn that it had a Milanese origin. This is apparent from the language used of St. Barnabas and St. Ambrose, patrons of Milan, one of whom is pointedly described as "Barnabas qui primus Mediolani missam celebravit," while the prayer commemorating the other was obviously penned under the shadow of the church of which he was archbishop. The information conveyed in the illuminated borders is more definite, proving beyond question that the MS. owed its existence to Bona of Savoy, wife of Galeazzo Maria, second Duke of Milan of the house of Sforza. Galeazzo, whose tyranny and vices had made him justly odious, was assassinated on 26th December, 1476. His widow then acted for a while as regent for her son Gian Galeazzo, who was only eight years of age; and some of the coins[1] struck for her in this capacity bear on the reverse the device of a phœnix rising from the flames, encircled with the motto, "Sola facta, solum Deum sequor." With the slight, and doubtless merely accidental, variation of "fata" for

---

[1] Gnecchi, *Le Monete di Milano*, 1884, p. 83, pl. xv. 2 ; Litta, *Famiglie Celebri Italiane*, Sforza pedigree, tab. v., no. 9.

"facta," both phœnix and motto form a conspicuous feature of the border reproduced here in pl. xlii. ; and, in addition to this, the words " Diva Bona" appear in several other borders (*e.g.*, ff. 66 *b*, 79 *b*, etc.), and "Bona Duc[issa]" is inscribed in extremely minute characters on the front of a building in the miniature of St. Clare (pl. xxiii.). Equally significant are the two initials B. M., which may be seen in pl. xxxviii. They are repeated elsewhere, and no doubt represent the names "Bona Maria," which in one instance are found written at length at the end of a psalm (f. 66) in order to fill up a line. Although she is almost invariably called by the first alone, both these names were in fact borne by the Duchess, who appears as Bona Maria in full, not only in the contemporary chronicle known as the "Diarium Parmense," but in some of her own letters and official documents as regent.[1]

The identity of the original owner of the MS. being thus placed beyond doubt, it remains to discover its more exact date and the special purpose, if any, for which so exceptionally choice a work of its kind was produced. From the device and motto above noticed, it was clearly completed after the tragedy that made the Duchess a widow; and there is additional evidence of this in the fact that St. Albert, one of the saints commemorated (pl. xviii.), was not canonized until 1476. Taking the extreme limits, its date therefore lies between 1477 and Bona's own death ; but, owing to the misfortunes of her later years, the actual period during which she was at all likely to have commanded the services of the first Milanese illuminators of the day was more narrowly circumscribed. Passionate, impulsive, and of no great ability, she was obviously ill-fitted for the difficult part she was called upon to play after her husband's death. It would seem, indeed, as if she had been specially marked out by fate to be the victim of a brother-in-law's unscrupulous ambition. Her elder sister having married Louis XI., she had been brought up as a girl at the Court of France ; and, before her union with Galeazzo Sforza in 1468, she narrowly missed becoming the

[1] Muratori, xxii., col. 249 ; *Archivio Storico Lombardo*, 1883, p. 315 ; C. Magenta, *I Visconti e gli Sforza nel castello di Pavia*, 1883, ii., p. 395.

wife of Edward IV. of England, as a pledge of amity between the two
nations.   This project, which is immortalized in Shakespeare's "Third
Part of King Henry VI.," was frustrated by Edward's infatuation
for Elizabeth Widvile; but, although Bona was thus rescued from
Richard of Gloucester, it was only to fall into the toils of a still greater
adept at intrigue and statecraft, her husband's second surviving brother,
Ludovico Sforza, surnamed Il Moro.   With the support of Galeazzo's
able minister, Cecco Simonetta, she nevertheless maintained her hold
of the regency until November, 1480, when, partly through her own
culpable folly, she was ousted by her wily antagonist.   Her first thought
after her fall was to take refuge in France, and, although foiled at the
time by Ludovico's jealousy, she is said to have made her way thither
in October, 1481, having spent the interval under mild restraint at
Abbiategrasso.   Her stay in France was, however, comparatively short.
Negotiations were opened by Louis on her behalf at least as early as
July, 1482,[1] and they ultimately resulted in her return to Milan, after
Louis himself was dead, at the end of 1483.   Probably the terms of
reconciliation, which included the restoring of her money and jewels,
were not very scrupulously observed; in any case, her life for the next
ten years was one of discomfort and chagrin, the scanty notices we have
of it showing her restless anxiety again to withdraw either to France or
to Savoy.   Although declared of full age, Duke Gian Galeazzo was in
fact a mere puppet in the hands of his uncle, whose policy was to keep
mother, as well as son, within his own control and surrounded by his
creatures.   In other respects, however, Bona appears to have been
treated with contemptuous indulgence, and she took a certain part as
Duchess-mother in the functions of the Court.   This was notably the
case at the marriages of the Duke with Isabel of Aragon in 1489, and
of her daughter Bianca Maria with the Emperor Maximilian I. in 1493.[2]
We hear of her again on 14th October, 1494, as receiving a visit from

---

[1] Morbio, *Storie dei Municipi Italiani*, 1840, p. 348; Rosmini, *Istoria di Milano*, 1820, iv., p. 221.
[2] "Nuptiæ Mediolanensium ducum," in *T. Chalchi Residua*, 1644, pp. 78, 108.

her nephew, Charles VIII. of France, when he passed through the Milanese borders on his foolish expedition to Naples.[1] She was then at Pavia, which just a week later was the scene of the premature death of her hapless son. Popular rumour, which accused Ludovico of having hastened the Duke's end by poison, possibly did him wrong ; but he did his best to justify it by openly usurping the dukedom to the exclusion of Gian Galeazzo's infant son. Under these circumstances Bona's lot was not likely to be any happier. Her treatment at this time is, in fact, curiously illustrated by a letter addressed to Ludovico from Antwerp, on 17th December, 1494, by Giovanni Cotta, secretary to the Empress Bianca Maria, the writer of which not only treacherously reports the bitter words used by her in venting her feelings to her daughter, but has the effrontery to add that, when reading to his mistress her mother's letters, he passed over all language of the kind and then immediately burnt them.[2] From this awkward position Bona did not succeed in extricating herself until December, 1495, when, on the demand of Charles VIII., and in spite of the Pope's influence being invoked to detain her, she was at length permitted to cross the Alps.[3] As she never returned to Milan, her subsequent movements do not so much concern us. Except that she was relieved from Ludovico's humiliating yoke, the change does not appear to have been much for the better ; for, although welcomed at first by Charles and provided with a pension, she almost immediately fell into neglect and obscurity. We catch glimpses of her, as "mal contenta et mal vista," at Tours, in April, 1496,[4] and vainly soliciting an audience with the King at Amboise four months later[5] ; and in January, 1499, she was at Lyons, apparently in want of means to carry her to Turin.[6] Her ultimate fate was long one

[1] Magenta, *op. cit.*, i., p. 531 ; H. F. Delaborde, *L'Expédition de Charles VIII. en Italie*, 1888, p. 418.
[2] F. Calvi, *Bianca Maria Sforza-Visconti*, 1888, p. 94.
[3] Rosmini, *op. cit.*, iv., p. 230.
[4] Marino Sanuto, *Diarii*, ed. N. Barozzi, 1879, i., col. 118.
[5] Rosmini, *op. cit.*, iv., p. 231.
[6] Morbio, *Codice Visconteo-Sforzesco*, 1846, p. 496, and *Municipi Italiani*, 1840, p. 350.

of the unsolved problems of history, but closer investigation[1] has now proved that she died on 17th November, 1503, in the castle of Fossano, which had been granted to her for a residence by her nephew Philibert, Duke of Savoy, on 21st April, 1500. Unhappily this tardy recognition of the claims of kinship did not secure her from being harassed by poverty to the very end. Milan was by this time in the power of the French, and Ludovico digesting the fruits of his ambition as a prisoner at Loches; and the state whose wealth had formerly supported her husband and herself in luxury and magnificence that were the wonder of Italy was now charged by Louis XII. with a miserable pittance on her behalf. Small as it was, however, it seems to have been irregularly paid, and probably the last letter she ever wrote, on 12th November, 1503, was a pathetic remonstrance on the subject.

The most obvious conclusion to be drawn from this brief recital of Bona's vicissitudes is that the MS. is antecedent in date to her fall from power in November, 1480. This might also be inferred perhaps from the " Diva Bona," which figures, as we have seen, in some of the borders, so adulatory an epithet naturally suggesting that her fortunes were not yet on the wane. For a parallel to it we need not go beyond the Sforza family. A striking instance of its use will be found in the set speech of Giasone del Maino, the Milanese ambassador, at Maximilian's reception of his new empress at Innsbruck on 16th March, 1494, where the orator in glorifying Ludovico, then at the height of his power, uniformly styles him " Divus Ludovicus."[2] On the other hand, there are considerations that make it, on the whole, more probable that the MS. really belongs to the later period, 1484–1494, when Bona, although deposed and slighted, still dwelt within the confines of Milan, and was presumably not yet debarred from indulging to some extent the

---

[1] G. Claretta, "Gli ultimi anni di Bona di Savoia," _Archivio Storico Italiano,_ 1870, p. 62.

[2] _Oratio Jasonis nitidissima in nuptias Maximiliani regis et Blancæ Mariæ reginæ Romanorum,_ Basel, 1494. It is a curious proof of Ludovico's ascendency in the state that the name of his nephew, the actual Duke and brother of the Empress, is not so much as mentioned.

sumptuous tastes that might be expected in Galeazzo Sforza's widow. Its artistic treatment certainly favours this view rather than the other. Both in design and execution, miniatures and borders alike present the characteristic Milanese style of the renaissance at its highest development, which was only attained under Ludovico il Moro, who, whatever his demerits, was a liberal patron of the arts. A splendid example, described and reproduced below (p. xxvii.), is furnished by the illuminated border round the first page of the "Sforziada," which is one of the treasures of the Grenville Library in the British Museum. This volume was printed at Milan in 1490, and to all appearance was Ludovico's own presentation-copy. The border therefore was no doubt painted at the same date, and, comparing it with those in Bona's Book of Hours, the resemblance in every way is so marked that a very few years at most can have separated them. It has accordingly been suggested[1] that the MS. was intended by Bona as a wedding-gift for her daughter, whose marriage to Maximilian was solemnized with great pomp at Milan on 30th November, 1493. Assuming that it must have been prepared for some such special occasion, this theory is a plausible one, but it is entirely unsupported by anything in the MS. itself. It rests mainly on the supposition that the initials B. M. stand for Bianca (not Bona) Maria.[2] There is, however, every reason to believe that this is not the case (above, p. iii.); and it is, moreover, a serious objection that among the infinitely varied decorative details it is impossible to detect the slightest allusion to an imperial alliance. This is the more remarkable as the marriage was one of which the upstart Sforzas were justifiably proud, and it is hardly credible that it should have been deliberately ignored in a work specially intended to celebrate it. The MS., indeed, is not in the same state as when it left the hands of the artists, and it is possible therefore that some evidence of the kind appeared on the missing leaves. As, however, no conceivable motive could have existed in this case for destroying every trace of it, such a solution is by no

---

[1] *Times* and *Guardian*, 24th May, 1893.
[2] Bianca (Blanca) Maria is in fact generally represented in similar cases by Bl. M.

means probable. It would be otherwise if the MS. had been really prepared in view of an abortive match, the memory of which it was desirable to obliterate. And, as a matter of fact, between 1487 and 1490 Bianca Maria was the affianced bride of John Corvinus, natural son and destined heir of Matthias, King of Hungary.[1] The sudden death of the elder Corvinus in 1490 nullified this scheme, for, when the son failed to secure the throne, Ludovico Sforza, who merely made use of his niece to further his ambition, at once turned elsewhere for a more suitable husband. The passion of Matthias for sumptuously decorated MSS. is notorious, and, had he survived and the marriage taken place, his daughter-in-law could have brought to Buda no more acceptable bridal-gift than a masterpiece of Milanese illumination ; and, moreover, if the volume was originally designed for this purpose and was still retained by Bianca Maria when she married Maximilian, a motive existed for its mutilation in the bitter hostility between Matthias and the house of Hapsburg, which renders it not unlikely that any allusion in it, by way of arms, device, or otherwise, to her projected union with his son would be carefully removed. But, if such was the case, the work of excision was not done so effectually as not to leave what may be taken as some slight evidence in support of this theory of origin ; for in a series of heroines depicted in the borders (below, p. xxv.) the only two of any apparent significance are Theodelind, Queen of the Lombards, and St. Elizabeth of Hungary. The main difficulty of the theory, of course, is to account for the neglect to fill up the consequent lacunæ at the time.

These, however, are only conjectures, and, so far as its own testimony goes, there is nothing to show that the MS. was not written and illuminated simply for Bona's own use and enjoyment. It would add to its interest if it could be identified with a Book of Hours of which a curious story is told in a letter printed in the *Archivio Storico Lombardo* for 1885, p. 541.[2] Unfortunately the date and address are

[1] Calvi, *op. cit.*, p. 10.
[2] In one of a series of valuable articles on "L'arte del minio nel ducato di Milano," compiled by G. Mongeri from notes of the Marchese Girolamo d'Adda.

not given, but the writer, who signs himself " Presbiter Johannes Petrus Biragus, Miniator," or illuminator, prays that a certain Frà Gian Jacopo, then in prison at Milan, might not be released until he had compensated him for the theft of an "Officiol imperfecto" which he had in hand for Bona the Duchess. The account given of the matter is not free from ambiguity, nor is the letter quite perfect. It appears, however, that a section of the MS. was in Bona's possession, and of the stipulated price 1220 "libre" still remained to be paid, while the stolen portion, valued at more than 500 ducats, had recently been presented to the person, apparently the titular or virtual head of the state, to whom the letter was addressed. From whom he obtained it we are not informed, but it had previously been taken by the thief to Rome and there sold to a friar, who in his turn had transferred it to "Monsignor Juan Maria Sforzino." The latter was a bastard half-brother of Galeazzo, Ascanio and Ludovico Sforza, and by the favour of Cardinal Ascanio was afterwards Archbishop of Genoa (1498–1513).[1] In the *Archivio* it is conjectured that Birago's appeal was made to Bona's husband, Duke Galeazzo, but it might equally well have been made some years later to Ludovico il Moro.[2] In the latter case there would be something like an agreement in date between the two MSS., and moreover, judging from its cost, Birago's, like the other, must have been of no ordinary kind.[3] Though it is impossible to conclude on such slight grounds that the two are identical, the letter at least deserves notice, since it not only shows Bona in the character of a patron, but gives the name of one of the illuminators whom she employed. There is other evidence of her artistic tastes in a letter to

[1] Marino Sanuto, *Diarii*, i., col. 925; Cappelletti, *Le Chiese d'Italia*, xiii., p. 377. The latter calls him a son of Galeazzo, but see Litta, tab. i.

[2] In his *Indagini sulla libreria Visconteo-Sforzesca*, 1875, i., p. 146, d'Adda, in fact, places it under the year 1490.

[3] From a recently discovered document (*Archivio Storico dell' Arte*, 1894, p. 59), it appears that Lionardo da Vinci's "Vierge aux Rochers" was valued at no more than 100 ducats, whereas the stolen portion of Birago's MS. was worth 500. The valuation in each case was the artist's own.

her from the Marquis Federigo Gonzaga, dated Mantua, 20th June, 1480, from which it appears that she had applied to no less famous a master than Mantegna to paint a miniature for her.[1]

To return to the Museum MS., although there is no internal evidence to connect it with Bianca Maria's marriage, there is a strong presumption from its after history that it was given to her at some time or other by her mother, and it may perhaps be the "Officiolum Mariæ Virginis" which is included in the wonderful inventory of her trousseau and all she took with her to Germany.[2] Assuming it to have belonged to the Empress, at her death without children in 1510 it would naturally pass to her husband Maximilian, who himself died early in 1519, leaving his grandson Charles, through his first wife Mary of Burgundy, as his heir. Already King of Spain and Sovereign of the Netherlands, Charles was elected Emperor as Charles V. on 28th June, 1519, and crowned on 23rd October, 1520. Whether by inheritance or otherwise, he certainly came into possession of the MS., and these dates are of special interest in connection with it, as coinciding with the time when it was completed in the state in which it now is. From whatever cause, its missing leaves had clearly been abstracted before this, and it is significant that the first of the substituted miniatures (pl. lv.) bears the date 1519, the very year in which the mutilated volume presumably descended to Charles V. from his grandfather. These miniatures, which will be discussed more at length later on, are all of the Flemish school and of the highest excellence. The more numerous inserted leaves that merely complete the text are of the same date. Two only of them

---

[1] Paris, Bibl. Nat., MS. Ital. 1592, no. 166. The same letter is evidently referred to by d'Adda and Mongeri in the *Arch. Stor. Lomb.*, 1885, p. 777, though the original is there said to be in a private collection. Bona's request moreover is erroneously stated to have been for a book of prayers ("Che gli miniasse un libro di preghiere"). The actual text runs :—"Ho ricevuto il ritracto de la pictura che la R.ᵐ vostra me ha mandato, et facto ogni instantia cum Andrea Mantegna mio pictore lo riduta ad elegante forma. El quale me dice che la saria opera piu presto da miniatore cha sua, perche lui non e assueto pingere figure picole, anzi assai meglio faria una nostra dona over qualche altra cosa de longeza de uno brazo aut uno brazo e mezo," etc.

[2] *Arch. Stor. Lomb.*, 1875, p.62. In Italian also in Calvi, *Bianca Maria Sforza-Visconti*, p. 133, "Uno officiolo de nostra Dona, cum le asse d'argento."

have borders (ff. 48, 213), which are in an imitative Italian style, while the text itself is in two or more hands, modelled on that of the original Italian scribe, but much less graceful and regular. The peculiar blackness of the ink in some places is a noteworthy feature. This is a characteristic of Spanish MSS., and, with some details in the miniatures, it suggests the probability that, although the style of art is essentially Flemish, the work of restoration was carried out in Spain or under strong Spanish influence. That Charles V. was intimately concerned with it is evident from the fact of his portrait being prominently introduced in one of the two later borders (pl. liv.). It is painted in gold on an oval medallion, with the date 1520 minutely inscribed on the rim and the initial K or monogram K.I., for "Karolus Imperator," four times repeated outside; and in its general treatment it strongly resembles the etched portrait of him by Jerome Hopfer, dated in the same year. As other books that belonged to him testify, he was not insensible to the charms of a fine illuminated MS., and it is not too violent an hypothesis that, on inheriting Bona's volume, he at once took steps to have its deficiencies made good. Be that as it may, the MS. undoubtedly took its final shape within the three years 1519-1521, the later limit being fixed by a prayer (f.253) in which Pope Leo X., who died on 1st December, 1521, is spoken of as still living. Its subsequent history, down to 1871, is unfortunately involved in obscurity.

Opinions may differ according to taste as to the relative superiority of the Italian and Flemish miniatures, but it will hardly be denied that they equally deserve to rank among the finest surviving examples of their respective schools. The full table of the subjects depicted is as follows, those treated by Flemish artists being marked by difference of type :—

1. St. John, f. 1.
2. St. Luke, f. 4.
3. St. Matthew, f. 7.
4. *St. Mark* (pl. lv.), f. 10 *b.*
5. *Christ nailed to the Cross,* f. 12 *b.*
6. The Descent of the Holy Spirit, f. 28.
7. *The Annunciation,* f. 41.
8. *The Visitation* (pl. lvi.), f. 61.
9. *The Adoration of the Angels at Bethlehem,* f. 82 *b.*
10. *The Shepherds at Bethlehem,* f. 91.
11. *The Adoration of the Magi* (pl. lvii.), f. 97.

The forty-eight Italian miniatures, as the earlier, claim the first attention. They are not all by the same hand, and nine in particular show a marked divergence in style from the rest. This is more especially the case with the first three, representing St. John, St. Luke, and St. Matthew, the designs of which are a little commonplace, though the colouring is rich. To a less extent the same may be said of the figures in the six which illustrate the Penitential Psalms (nos. 56-61), but the landscape backgrounds, with their curious arrangement of rocks piled one on another (*cf.* pl. xxiv.), are more effective. No plate of any of these nine subjects is here given, the facsimiles being limited to those of the highest artistic merit and best adapted to a mechanical process of reproduction. The remaining thirty-nine are more nearly on a level, and, if not actually by a single artist, are of precisely the same school. Generally speaking, the grouping is good, the figures well proportioned and animated, and the features full of expression. Though occasionally too redundant, the loose draperies are disposed in natural folds, free from undue stiffness. The hair, which is nearly always light in colour, is characteristically treated, mostly falling in long ringlets or being crisply curled. These and other points may be judged from the facsimiles, but, though the designs are preserved, the colouring is necessarily sacrificed. Both in the miniatures and borders, except where the edges have been slightly rubbed, this is to all appearance as fresh as when it was first laid on, and its richness and brilliancy are extraordinary, so much so, indeed, that the effect, it must be confessed, is in some cases too glaring to be wholly agreeable. The predominant tints are blue, generally a deep ultramarine, red and green in various shades, and a pale canary-yellow ; but russet-brown, grey and black, and, more rarely, lilac, violet, and lake are also employed. To judge from the shiny surface, the pigments were probably mixed in a weak solution of gum-arabic. The yellow is invariably shaded with red, and a fine effect is produced with red and brown by delicately heightening them with gold. By this means, for example, even the dingy Franciscan habit is suffused with a fine glow. Otherwise gold is on the whole sparingly used, the miniature of St. Gregory being the most notable exception ; it is thinly applied through a liquid medium, and is never burnished.

Of the series of nine miniatures depicting scenes of the Passion (nos. 17–25), five are here reproduced. In pl. i., the Payment of Judas, the traitor wears a green robe, and a pale yellow mantle lined with blue ; the youth who is telling out the coins has a blue tunic, red under-sleeves and wallet, pale yellow hose, and blue boots ; and the seated figure, a red robe, blue hanging sleeves, a red hood lined with white, and a

blue skull-cap.   The remaining figures are in red, blue and green.[1]   It
may be noticed in passing that the Flemish artist who painted the
Entry into Jerusalem on the opposite page evidently worked with this
miniature before him, the strongly marked Jewish features of Judas, as
well as his costume, being exactly copied.   Pl. ii., the Last Supper, is
in all points one of the finest miniatures in the whole MS., the finish
given to the features being especially noticeable.   Our Lord is clothed
in a red robe with the high lights in gold, a small portion of a blue
mantle being visible over His left shoulder.   On His right is seated
St. Peter, who wears a green robe edged with gold and a mantle of blue
lined with yellow ; while St. John on the other side is in paler green,
with a red mantle lined with blue.   Judas is habited as in pl. i., the
apostle on his right in a red robe and a blue mantle lined with green ;
the rest are in various combinations of the same colours as those already
specified.   Of the servitors in the foreground, the one on the left has a
blue tunic and red hose, the other a light green tunic, blue under-sleeves,
a crimson belt, and pale yellow hose.   The floor is green, the panels
of the balustrade alternately dark green and crimson, with borders of
light blue and an outer framework of gold.   The servitor in the rear
stands in front of a curtain of myrtle green studded and bordered with
gold ; he wears a crimson tunic, open at the neck and showing blue
beneath.   Like the rest, he has a white stole worn deacon-wise over the
left shoulder.   All the table utensils are of dull gold, as are also the
nimbi.   That of Judas, however, is an exception, being coloured a light
brown.   In the small subsidiary scenes in the upper corners the backgrounds are in shades of blue, the figures in red, blue and green.   As
in other cases, they are less carefully executed than the main subject,
and were perhaps put in by a pupil.   Pl. iii., Christ before Annas, may
also be the work of a different hand, together with the two miniatures
on either side of it in the above list.   Our Lord wears a robe of clear
light blue, showing a red lining at the wrists.   Annas, whose bloated

[1] The word at the foot of the page, in this and other cases, is the initial word of the
accompanying lesson or prayer.   The letters are in gold on a blue or crimson ground.

features recall some of the grotesque designs of Lionardo, is also in blue, with loose sleeves and hood of yellow, the latter being lined with grey ; while the figure holding the pastoral staff has a blue skirt and red bodice, with sleeves from the elbow of green slashed with white. Pl. iv., the Crucifixion, does not do adequate justice to what is really a fine and harmonious composition, the impression of confusion and overcrowding which it may be thought to convey being largely due to the loss of the colouring. The soldiers in the foreground wear dark bronze-like armour ; the one on the left has moreover a pale yellow surcoat and green sleeves, the one on the right a green surcoat and blue sleeves and cap, and the third a blue surcoat and red sleeves, while our Lord's garment for which they are casting lots is a clear blue. The Virgin's robe is of red shot with gold, her mantle and hood of blue lined with green ; St. John, as before, is in green, with a mantle of red lined with blue. In the beautiful Deposition from the Cross (pl. v.) the Virgin is similarly clothed ; the other women, beginning on the left, are in green and blue lined with red, red and yellow lined with green, and blue and yellow lined with green. Nicodemus behind is in blue and red, Joseph of Arimathæa in yellow and blue ; the mantles of both being lined with green. In the background are the Harrowing of Hell and the Resurrection, not in separate compartments (*cf.* pl. iii.), but forming part, as it were, of the same picture.

In the miniatures of Saints there is naturally more scope for variety of treatment ; and their landscape settings, though deficient in atmosphere and without the exquisitely soft effects of distance which impart such a charm to the productions of the Flemish school, are often of singular interest. In nearly all cases, the trees and rocks are purely conventional, the former being generally rounded in form and of a sombre hue. The architectural features, on the contrary, are highly realistic (*e.g.*, pl. vi., xi., xx.) ; while the foregrounds and the water which is nearly always introduced in the middle distance are skilfully treated. The sky is a clear blue, with light fleecy clouds of white or gold, toning down towards the horizon into a lighter blue or

greenish yellow (*e.g.*, pl. vii.).   A characteristic feature in many cases
is the presence in the foreground of formal stumps of trees cut off
cleanly near to the ground.   They are especially observable in the
miniatures, such as pl. xx. and that of St. Jerome (no. 40), which in
other respects most nearly resemble the series of the Penitential Psalms,
where they are equally in evidence.   It may be noticed also that the
loose stones which often cover the ground are brightly tinted so as to
look almost like jewels.

By the aid of the list above the subjects of most of the miniatures
are easily recognizable ; a few of the designs, however, need explana-
tion, and others for various reasons may be briefly noticed.   In
pl. vi., commemorating the Assumption, the Virgin is in white shaded
with grey, while the cherubs who surround her are in a halo of gold.
The angel on the left is in green, with wings, sleeves, and collar of
red shot with gold ; the other angel is in the same colours reversed.
St. Michael, in pl. vii., wears a deep blue surcoat over a violet tunic,
which is seen only at the shoulders and below his golden armour ; his
wings are of green, violet, and crimson heightened with gold ; his legs
are bare as far as the boots, which are of lake.   The fiend on whom
he is trampling is coloured green, spotted with gold, his wings,
however, being red.   Pl. viii., the Baptism of our Lord, is remarkable
for its luminosity and vivid colouring, more particularly the blue of the
sky and stream, of our Lord's garments borne by the angel on the
left, and of the robe of the angel holding the cross.   The Baptist is
richly clad in a robe of red and gold, lined with pale green.   In pl. ix.
the scene represented is the baptism by St. James the Greater of
Josias, the officer who was leading him to execution, but was converted
on the way and condemned to suffer with him.   The saint is clad in
blue, with a mantle of red and gold lined with green.   The kneeling
figures wear loose drapery of pale yellow and white respectively ; the
elderly man on the left is in blue and crimson, the soldier in green and
gold.   The dwarf on the right has blue hose, and a red and gold tunic
open in front and showing a dark green vest ; the executioner wears

a brick-red jacket with ragged under-sleeves of pale green; and the figure behind St. James has a blue turban, a blue robe lined with red, and a green under-garment. In the Martyrdom of St. Sebastian (pl. x.) the saint has a cincture of pale yellow; the judge a robe of red and gold turned up at the wrists with white, and a blue hood. The chair on which he sits is of green bordered with gold, and the steps leading up to it are of the same colours faced with crimson. The two archers in the foreground wear blue tunics and bright red hose, the foremost one also having golden shoulder-pieces, red sleeves slashed with white, and blue boots; and the bearded archer behind has a green tunic and red vest, with pale yellow hose. In pl. xi. the very youthful St. George is clad in golden armour and a blue surcoat; his under-sleeves are red and his boots red turned up with blue. Before him kneel the king and queen, the former in red and gold, with a blue collar and under-sleeves; while on the right the rescued princess, in a blue robe with red sleeves and floating drapery of pale yellow, leads the dragon by a golden ribbon. The tamed monster is painted dark green and gold, with crimson and blue on his wings.

The miniature reproduced in pl. xii. is perhaps the most brilliant in colouring of all. St. Gregory is robed in white and scarlet; the curtain behind him is of gold, the desk of gold, crimson and light blue. The acolytes on either side wear long blue robes, the collars and under-sleeves from the elbow being of green. The wall behind is a rich myrtle green, the windows of pale blue glass framed in lake, the bound volumes crimson and blue; the floor is green, the steps crimson bordered with gold, and the initial word "Concede" gold on a blue ground. Pl. xiii. represents the baptism of St. Augustine by St. Ambrose at Milan, in A.D. 387. The nimbus of the officiating saint, who is vested in an alb and a crimson cope lined with green, is just visible behind his mitre. St. Augustine has a cincture of pale yellow; the cassocks and stoles of the clergy and others are of light blue or scarlet; the second figure on the left, holding the pastoral staff, is in pale yellow, and the other behind St. Augustine on his left in blue. The subject of pl. xiv.

d

is well known, and has been treated by some of the most famous artists, Raphael and Murillo included. The story ran that, while meditating his treatise on the Trinity, St. Augustine one day came upon a Child seated on the shore and professedly trying to empty the ocean into a hole which He had dug in the sand. Naturally he pointed out that the task was futile, when the Child promptly retorted that it was not more so than the attempt to explain the mystery of the divine nature. The nimbus round the Child's head here identifies Him, as in other cases, with Christ Himself; and the allusion is still further emphasized by the semblance of the Trinity suspended in the sky. St. Bernard's Vision of the Virgin (pl. xv.) has also been a favourite subject with artists, and its treatment here is a pleasing example. The saint, who wears a black habit, is accompanied by his emblem, a chained demon, whose body is of dark brown heightened with gold and his wings of blue. The desk and seat are of crimson picked out with gold and bordered with gold and blue; and the floor is composed of green, violet and yellow tiles.

Unlike the rest, the saint commemorated in pl. xvi. is of doubtful identity. In the accompanying prayer, indeed, he is styled "Henricus Pontifex," but the only bishop of the name generally recognized as a saint in the hagiologies is Henry, Bishop of Upsal and apostle of the Finns (d. 1157), whose presence in an Italian Book of Hours is extremely improbable. There is a possible alternative in Henry, Archbishop of Reims (d. 1175), an ardent disciple of St. Bernard, whose miniature immediately precedes. Although never actually canonized, he appears to have been admitted to the preliminary degree of a "Beatus,"[1] and, as son of Louis VI. of France and Adelaide of Savoy, he was not only a member of the royal house with which Bona of Savoy had intimate relations, but belonged to her own family. St. Louis, however, a far more illustrious saint, might equally have claimed her devotion on the same grounds; and, comparing the kneeling group

---

[1] He is to find a place in the *Acta Sanctorum*, when the work reaches the 15th Dec. (*De prosecutione operis Bollandiani*, 1838, p. 37). Another Henry who is called "Beatus" was Abbot of Clairvaux and Cardinal-Bishop of Albano (d. 1189).

here with that in pl. xviii., it would seem as if the bishop depicted was
specially a healer of the sick.   But, whatever its motive, the miniature
is one of great richness and beauty.   The saint is sumptuously robed
in episcopal vestments of deep blue bordered with gold and lined with
crimson.   The angel in the foreground is in blue, with under-sleeves
of pale yellow and wings of gold ; the angel behind has a robe and
wings of red and gold, with under-sleeves of green.   The kneeling
figure in front wears a blue tunic, and a red cloak lined with green ; the
woman next to him is in pale blue, and the man on her right in red.
The peacock, which is exquisitely painted, is probably a mere ornamental accessory and not St. Henry's particular emblem.   In pl. xvii.,
however, the two arrows lying on the ground identify St. Giles even
without the rubric, "Oratio S. Gilii Abbatis."   He is not often represented in Italian art, but is here depicted in an alb and a cope of red
and gold, lined with blue.   The angel on the left has a pale yellow
skirt and sleeves and a blue bodice ; the one on the right a light blue
skirt and sleeves and a light green bodice ; the wings of both are of red
tinged with gold.   St. Albert of Trapani (pl. xviii.), on the contrary, was
essentially an Italian saint ; moreover, he is the latest commemorated in
the MS., not having been canonized until 1476.   He appears in the
brown and white garb of a Carmelite, an angel on either side, clad in pale
green with wings and sleeves of red and gold, bearing his emblems, a lily
and an open book.   He is called in the rubric "Liberator a febribus,"
and there is a marked contrast between the two kneeling groups.   Those
on the right are pale and emaciated with fever, and have their heads
swathed in linen bandages ; the boy wears a pale green tunic and blue
hose, the man is in pale yellow with green hose, and the woman in light
blue.   The others, whom he is addressing, appear to have been cured,
and have the hue of health.   The child is in white, the woman next him
in a light blue dress, the full sleeves being pale yellow and the close-
fitting under-sleeves green edged with gold ; while the second woman has
a red dress, and green sleeves slashed with white.   The more subdued
tones and pleasing design of this miniature render it peculiarly effective.

The subject of pl. xix., St. Peter Martyr the Dominican being slain by assassins on the way from Como to Milan, and writing the initial word of the Creed on the ground with his blood, is common enough, and there is no special point of interest in its treatment. Only one of the assassins is introduced, who cleaves the saint's skull with one sword while he stabs his companion friar with another. The two Dominicans wear the black and white habit of their order. The assassin has a close-fitting blue jacket, with white at the neck and elbow ; his belt and shoulder-tags are red and gold, and his boots green ; his hose is parti-coloured, the right leg being yellow and blue, the left crimson and grey. In pl. xx., we have the founder himself of the rival order, St. Francis of Assisi, represented in the act of receiving the stigmata, the seraphic figure, whose folded wings are blood-red, hovering above. Another Franciscan saint appears in pl. xxi., the famous preacher and reformer of the order, St. Bernardino of Siena, who was canonized in 1450, six years after his death. Like St. Francis himself, he wears the brown habit and hood, heightened with gold; in his hand he carries his emblem, a tablet bearing on a blue ground the name IHS. within a circle of golden rays. The two friars in front are in brown, the other two in black, the mitres they are offering him typifying the three bishoprics which he refused, viz. Siena, Fermo and Urbino.

St. Catharine of Siena, in pl. xxii., is the second of four female saints, who complete the series. While the older St. Catharine of Alexandria is depicted in the preceding miniature as rescued from the wheel by a storm of stones and fire from heaven, her Italian namesake appears in a character common to both, as the spiritual bride of the Saviour receiving from Him the ring of espousal. In this charming composition both our Lord and His mother wear a red robe and blue mantle, that of our Lord showing a green lining. St. Catharine and St. Dominic, the founder of the order to which she belonged, are in black and white, while King David, who stands behind the Virgin, has a red robe with blue collar. The two saints on the left are apparently St. Paul and St. John ; the former is in red and blue, the latter in blue with a mantle of pale yellow lined with light green. The same grace and refinement that characterize the figure of St. Catharine are equally conspicuous in the group of nuns in the miniature of St. Clare (pl. xxiii.), who is repelling a Saracen attack upon her convent of St. Damiano near Assisi by holding up the Monstrance or Pyx. In common with her attendant nuns, she wears a black or dark grey gown and a brown cloak heightened with gold, with a white coif and black hood. The kneeling soldier has a dark green surcoat spotted with gold, and blue sleeves and boots; the other has a blue surcoat, and red sleeves and boots; the armour of both being a dark bronze-like gold. The Assumption of St. Mary Magdalen (pl. xxiv.) is another example of resplendent colour. Against a deep blue sky she is seen rising to heaven, covered only with the rippling masses of her bright golden hair, which is painted with marvellous skill. Of the four angels who support her, the two uppermost have flowing drapery of golden brown, pale yellow sleeves, and red wings shot with gold; the others have red and gold drapery, dark blue sleeves, and golden brown wings. Below, on the right is the hermit who witnessed the Assumption; on the left is a scene which alludes to one of the Magdalen's most famous miracles. The wife of a Gallic prince having died in childbirth on the way to the Holy Land, her husband left the corpse, together with the newly born infant, on a desert island, commending them to the care of the saint. Touching again at the island on his return, he saw a child playing on the shore, and on following it into a cave found his wife restored to life.

The Death of the Virgin (pl. xxv.), which has a place in the Office of the Dead, is an interesting design, and is finely coloured. The Virgin's cloak and hood are a deep blue, the opening where the hands are crossed showing a red garment underneath. The apostle kneeling in the foreground has a yellow robe, and a blue mantle lined with green; and, like St. Peter on the further side of the couch, he is wearing a very modern-looking pince-nez. St. Peter, who is using the asperge, is vested in a blue cassock, an alb, and a rich violet cope, the border of which is of gold, studded with jewels ; while the two apostles next to him on either side are in green and red, and red and green, respectively, the mantle in each case being lined with blue. The coverlet of the couch is of red heightened with gold ; the "Venite" is on a blue ground ; and the floor-tiles are dark green and slate-blue.

The Italian borders are in several different hands, those between ff. 45 and 127, with some striking exceptions (e.g., pl. xxxv.–xli.), being generally inferior to the rest. The grounds are mostly rich crimson, blue, and myrtle green, the same panel often containing all three colours, two disposed in vertical bands, and the third filling up the spaces enclosed within the ornamental designs. These designs are painted in gold and softly modulated tones of light blue, green, violet, and grey ; and many of them for fertility of invention and perfection of finish could hardly be surpassed. They exhibit an infinite variety of the beautiful arabesques characteristic of the renaissance, in which vases, trophies and candelabra, delicate foliage, flowers and scroll-work, griffins, fawns, sphinxes, and other fanciful creatures, amorini in all attitudes, medallions containing portrait-busts or exquisite copies of antique gems,[1] and cunningly simulated pearls, rubies and emeralds, are harmoniously inter-mingled. In no case does the scroll-work extend beyond the straight line of the border, nor are there any of the spots of burnished gold with radiating filaments common in Italian MSS. of other schools at this period ; and, although the colours are bright, the general effect is one of richness rather than extreme brilliancy. At the head and foot of the page small miniatures are usually introduced. The subjects depicted are sometimes independent, such as birds and beasts, among which a partiality is shown for the dove, white rabbit, and ermine, the first two, at least, being recognized Sforza emblems. There are, however, several instances in which the miniatures form a series, having a more or less appropriate reference to the text. The first of these series, running

---

[1] One of the subjects (f. 109 b) is the well-known one of Diomed holding the Palladium (*Jahrb. des Kaiserl. Deutsch. Archäol. Instituts*, Berlin, iii., 1888, p. 220, tab. viii. 2).

through the Hours of the Holy Cross (ff. 13-27), gives the symbols of
the Passion in the upper compartments; while in the lower ones
patriarchs, apostles, and saints, beginning with Isaac, Peter, Barnabas,
and Paul, are curiously represented by naked amorini carrying an
emblem or other indication of identity, with the name generally
written in the corner, as may be seen in plates xxvi. and xxvii. A still
finer series of eighteen miniatures illustrates the Hours of the Holy
Spirit (ff. 29-39), the subjects of which are richly draped angels playing
on musical instruments. The forms of the various instruments are not
the least interesting feature of the design. They include, among others,
a lute played with a plectrum (f. 29), a bagpipe (f. 31 b), a hurdy-gurdy
(f. 32), a monochord with a bow (f. 32 *b*), a clarinet with a bladder
(f. 34), a curved horn, or cornetto, pierced with holes (f. 34 *b*), a pan-pipe
also pierced with holes (f. 36), a pipe, and a monochord with a hammer
(f. 36 *b*), a dulcimer (f. 37), and a psaltery (f. 38). Six pages of this
series are here reproduced (plates xxviii.-xxxiii.). Among them, the
border in pl. xxix. has a miniature with a ground of dark green spotted
with gold; the angel has a blue robe, with under-sleeves of pale green
and wings of crimson shot with gold. In pl. xxx. the ground is dark
crimson; the angel's robe is of sage green, his under-sleeves of crimson,
his wings of light blue, green, and red. The wings of the angel in
pl. xxxi. are also of three colours, lake, blue, and green; her dress is of
red and gold, her collar and under-sleeves of green, while the ground of
the miniature is of dark blue. Crimson again forms the background of
pl. xxxii., but the angel's wings, together with the bands crossed on his
breast and the psaltery on which he is playing, are of plain gold; his
dress is of soft grey, the sleeves pale blue, and the collar pale green.

The page figured in pl. xxxv. is one of several in this part of the MS.
which differ in character from the rest in having the text not enclosed
within the ordinary form of border, consisting of four rectangular panels,
but suspended, as it were, in front of an architectural framework. The
border immediately preceding (f. 51) is the best in this style, but the
attempt to reproduce it satisfactorily was unsuccessful. It has a

charming amorino standing on either side, and in the compartment at
the bottom two sphinxes and a fine Mantegnesque Medusa-like head. In
the border here given the background is a somewhat disagreeable tone
of blue, the framework is of gold picked out with crimson, and the
candelabra of gold shaded with grey. The ornamentation on the top
is also in grey, together with the two masks, which are on a crimson
ground bordered by bands of blue. The chief attraction of the page,
however, is the charming bust of a young girl, which is exquisitely
painted on a black ground. Her complexion is a clear blonde, strings
of pearls are entwined in her light golden hair, and red drapery
touched with gold is about her shoulders. This bust might perhaps be
thought to represent Bianca Maria Sforza. It bears, however, little
resemblance to her fine portrait in the Brera at Milan, formerly
attributed to Lionardo da Vinci, but by Morelli to Ambrogio de Predis[1];
and it is not improbably copied from a gem of the younger Faustina.[2]
In decorative effect the border in pl. xxxvi. is far superior. The
ground of this is of crimson, the ornamentation merely of gold and
tender shades of grey, while the peacocks are in their natural colours,
wonderfully rendered. In the small miniature at the foot of the page
the ground is black starred with gold, within a border of blue ; the
saint is clothed in light blue, with a mantle of red relieved with gold.
Equally effective combinations of crimson, gold and grey are found in
plates xxxviii. and xli., slight touches of blue and green being added
in the former and the initials B. M. standing on a blue ground. In
plates xxxvii., xxxix. and xl., on the contrary, the grounds are brilliantly
parti-coloured ; and the medallion-busts, amorini and jewels are especially
noticeable for artistic beauty and finish. In pl. xxxvii. the small cameo
on the right has some likeness to the profile of Gian Galeazzo, as
engraved on his coins[3]; and the bust in pl. xl., which, together with the

---

[1] See the frontispiece of Calvi's *Bianca Maria Sforza-Visconti*, 1888, aud Müntz,
La Renaissance, 1885, p. 223.

[2] See Bernoulli, *Die Bildnisse der Römischen Kaiser*, 1891, ii., tab. iv. 8.

[3] Gnecchi, *Le Monete di Milano*, table xvi.

oval plaque, is in gold, is possibly intended for Bona herself. The interest of pl. xlii. lies mainly in the device and motto (see above, p. ii). These are painted on a blue ground ; the phœnix being of gold, with wings touched with red, blue and green. Otherwise the border, like others in its immediate neighbourhood, is comparatively poor in design.

With the Prayers on the Passion a better hand again takes up the decoration, the colours being deeper and richer in tone, and the designs more delicately elaborated ; and from this point to the end of the MS. the borders, though more artists than one have apparently contributed, are uniformly of the highest order. The above prayers occupy five pages only, the border of each including one or more incidents of the Passion. An example, which is perhaps the finest of the series, may be seen in pl. xliii. After this comes a long break, the only border remaining between f. 170 and f. 247 being the later one (f. 213, pl. liv.) in which is the portrait of Charles V. The next series, which begins on f. 251, closely resembles in treatment that dealing with the Passion. In it are introduced finely executed figures of Biblical and other heroines and female saints. Those that survive are Deborah, " Ducissa et prophetissa"; Esther, "regis Asueri uxor"; Judith, "quæ amputavit caput Holofernis"; Anna, "vidua et prophetissa"; "Theodorina" (or Theodelind), Queen of the Lombards; St. Pelagia, "quæ monacalem sumpsit habitum"; and St. Elizabeth of Hungary. The special motive for the not wholly complimentary selection of St. Pelagia is hard to conjecture.

The Office of the Dead, which has only one full-page miniature (pl. xxv.), is decorated in compensation with no less than forty-one borders, the number no doubt having originally been larger still. The small miniatures in some of them have no apparent relation to the subject-matter of the text, including, for example, a stag, a lion devouring a pig, a dog catching a hare, an amorino playing the violin, and a pretty centaur-like creature, half-amorino, half-deer. Many on the contrary exhibit amorini contemplating or sporting with human skulls, or struggling with serpents, together with various emblems of mortality ; while a phœnix

c

(f. 271 *b*) serves both for the device of Bona of Savoy and for a type of the Resurrection.   In pl. xliv. the ground of the side-panels is blue, with crimson within the angles formed by the cross-bones ; the dragon-like creatures are green and gold ; the larger square jewels are rubies and the smaller ones emeralds.   The ground at the top is crimson, the portion round the skull being green.   The ermines below, enclosed within a fence, no doubt bear some special significance as a device, and they not only appear in other borders, but in several of the full-page miniatures, notably in the first of all and in the Penitential Psalms series.   In pl. xlv. the panel on the left has vertical bands of blue and crimson, with green between in the enclosed spaces ; that on the right is in crimson and green, with blue between.   The panel at the top is blue ; the eagle, as well as the cockatrice below, is of gold.   For softness and grace none of the pages excel that in pl. xlix.   The outer vertical bands are of crimson, the inner of green, while the spaces within the horns of the ox-skulls, between the winged grotesques, and round the shells at the bottom are of dark blue.   The shells, grotesques and serpents are of dull gold, as well as the dragons at the top, which are on a crimson ground.   The sleeping lion is of golden brown ; out of his ear creeps a weasel, while another is climbing over his back. Probably this also forms a device, but there is no evidence to show to whom it belongs.   In pl. li. the illuminator has taken his motive more directly from the text than usual, illustrating Ps. xii., " Blessed is he that considereth the poor."   The ground of the miniature is of blue ; the jewel upon it is a ruby, set in gold and surrounded with pearls and emeralds.   The young man's doublet is of gold shaded with red, his under-sleeves light blue slashed with white, his cap bright scarlet ; the beggar wears a garment of light brick-red.   The single figure of pl. lii. stands out well against a background of crimson with golden stars ; her dress is of golden brown, relieved with white along the sleeves.   This page and still more that in pl. liii. strongly recall the hand which executed the series of angel-musicians in the earlier part of the MS.   The three angels in pl. liii. illustrate the " Cantate " of the text.   The one on either side is in pale yellow, with under-sleeves of gold ; the third is in light blue. The wings of all three, and of the angel at the top of the page, are of gold ; the volume from which they are reading is bound in crimson. The ground of the miniature, as well as of that at the top of the page, is of blue. The angel playing the violin is robed in white, with sleeves of red and gold.

To name with any approach to certainty the artists by whom these exquisite miniatures and borders were painted is, in our present state of knowledge, impossible ; and it is partly in the hope of obtaining more light on this interesting question by facilitating comparison with other examples in Italy and elsewhere that the present selection of plates has been issued. Materials for satisfactory comparison near at hand are unfortunately rare, the Milanese school of illumination not being so well represented in England as its Florentine rival. The British Museum, however, is fortunate enough to possess two other contemporary specimens of the highest importance. One of these is the border, already mentioned (p. vii.), in the printed Sforziada,[1] or Life of Francesco Sforza-Visconti, fourth Duke of Milan, translated into Italian from the Latin of Giovanni Simonetta by Christophoro Landino, and published at Milan in 1490. This border has been photographed on a reduced scale in pl. lxi., the details being repeated in their actual size in plates lxii.–lxv. ; but it is only when the original is examined side by side with the actual borders in the MS. that the full force of the resemblance can be realized, embracing, as it does, not only the designs, but the peculiar tones and arrangement of the colours. The narrow panel on the left especially (pl. lxiv.) might have been transferred almost bodily from the MS. The ground, like so many there, is formed of two vertical bands of green and blue, with crimson within the enclosed spaces, and the same delicate tints of blue,

---

[1] *Historia delle cose facte dallo invictissimo duca Francesco Sforza scripta in Latino da Giovanni Simonetta et tradocta in lingua Fiorentina da Christophoro Landino Fiorentino ;* with the colophon, "Questa Sfortiada . . . la impressa Antonio Zarotto Parmesano in Milano nelli anni del Signore MCCCCLXXXX."

green and grey relieve the gold of the design. The broader panel on
the right (pl. lxv.) has an outer band of blue and an inner one of
crimson, the enclosed spaces being a dark green. The dragons are of
blue, toning to light green underneath and stippled with gold, while
the human figures issuing from their mouths, after the manner of the
well-known "biscia" of the Visconti arms, are of red heightened with
gold. The body of the vase is of gold; the designs running round it
are on grounds of blue and crimson, and the leaf-moulding is light blue
and green. The faces and breasts of the two sphinxes are in flesh
tints, their bodies, limbs and wings of shaded gold. The golden-
winged angel above the medallion is clad in light blue, with a collar of
red and gold and golden bands across the chest; her under-sleeves,
together with the tunic of the amorino below, are in the same pale
canary-yellow shaded with red which is so common in Bona's Book of
Hours. In the panel at the top of the page (pl. lxii.) the darker ground
is of crimson, the lighter of green; the flowers are light blue and grey.
The Moor's head, an obvious allusion to Ludovico il Moro, is on a blue
ground, the drapery about his shoulders being a light yellow. The
sportive amorini in pl. lxiii. form a delightful group, those on the left
being engaged in the Italian equivalent of the child's game of "Hot
Cockles," and those on the right in that of "Buck, buck, how many horns
do I hold up?" The sward on which they stand is dark green relieved
with gold, the background a deep blue studded with golden stars;
and their wings are of crimson heightened with gold. In the centre
is Ludovico Sforza's shield of arms, resplendent with *or* and *argent*,
azure and *gules*, with the lilies of France on an escutcheon of pretence.
It has the same quarterings as in Add. MS. 21,413 (see below), where,
however, it is impaled with the arms of Beatrice d'Este, his wife. On
the impaled side here will be observed the "spazzola," or brush, with
the motto "Merito et tempore." This is introduced also in the side
panels, and is found on some of Ludovico's coins [1]; but, as it was used

---

[1] Gnecchi, *Le Monete di Milano*, pp. lxxv., 89, and pl. xvi., 6.

by his father and brother before him,[1] the stories told by Giovio and others to account for his adoption of it are no doubt mere inventions. The two admirably painted and life-like portrait-busts have still to be considered. They are painted on a blue ground decorated with gold, and represent Duke Francesco Sforza and Ludovico il Moro his son. Francesco's portrait, which bears his name, was perhaps taken from a fine medal, having partly the same inscription, which is engraved by Litta. If there is any doubt as to the identity of the other,[2] it need only be compared with the portrait of Ludovico in the well-known picture, now said to be by Bernardino de' Conti, in the Brera at Milan, where he is kneeling with his wife and children before the Virgin.[3] The costumes of father and son here are alike, consisting of steel armour with a linked collar of gold. Each, however, wears on the breast his own special emblem, that of Francesco being hardly so distinguishable in the original as in the plate. All that can be seen of it is a greyhound seated beneath a tree ; but in other places where it occurs, as in the medal above, in many of the Sforza MSS. at Paris,[4] and in a picture of Francesco and his wife in the church of San Sigismondo near Cremona, there is also a hand issuing from a cloud, with or without a dog-collar. Ludovico's emblem, on the contrary, consists of two high towers, perhaps intended for the pillars of Hercules, with water flowing between them ; and the same is repeated on a shield lower

---

[1] Zanetti, *Nuova raccolta delle monete*, Bologna, 1774, i., 218 ; Paris, Bibl. Nat., MSS. Lat. 7709 (A.D. 1459) and 8550 (A.D. 1472), MS. Ital. 973 (A.D. 1473), and many others.

[2] Dibdin (*Bibl. Decameron*, iii., p. 176), H. Shaw (*Illuminated Ornaments*, 1833, no. xxxv.), and even Mr. J. W. Bradley (*Dict. of Miniaturists*, 1889, iii., p. 232), unaccountably take it to represent Card. Ascanio Sforza. Shaw's coloured facsimile of part of the border, including the portrait, by no means does it justice.

[3] See the plate in Kugler, *Handbook of Painting, Ital. Schools*, 1887, ii., p. 385. There is also a photograph in Delaborde's *Exp. de Charles VIII. en Italie*, 1888, p. 274, where it is attributed to Zenale.

[4] On his expulsion of Ludovico from Milan Louis XII. seized the Sforza library in the castle of Pavia, and many of the volumes are now in the Bibliothèque Nationale (Delisle, *Le Cabinet des MSS.*, i., p. 125 ; Mazzatinti, *MSS. Ital. delle Biblioteche di Francia*, 1886, i., p. lxv. ; d'Adda, *Indagini*, i., p. xviii.).

down in the border, as well as in another Sforziada, which is preserved in the Bibliothèque Nationale.

The Paris Sforziada here mentioned is a companion volume to that in the Museum, being the same Milan edition of 1490, and similarly printed on vellum.[1] The corresponding border, however, is somewhat differently treated, and, whereas Francesco Sforza's portrait is almost a replica, instead of Ludovico's it gives us the refined and melancholy features of the young Duke Gian Galeazzo. At the foot of the page uncle and nephew appear together in an allegorical design. In the foreground they are facing one another on the margin of the sea or, more probably perhaps, of Lake Maggiore ; each is kneeling on one knee and pointing upwards towards the portrait of Francesco, founder of their line, and below are the inscriptions " Patrem et patrem patriae veneremur " and " Merito utrique teneor ; dedit ille, tu conserva," the latter sentence of course being put into the mouth of Gian Galeazzo. Again, on the water behind them rides a vessel borne onward by a favouring breeze ; Gian Galeazzo stands or kneels amidship, with his hands extended as if in prayer, while in the stern sits a Moor, holding both steering-oar and sheets, and on the horizon, as a kind of merman, St. Louis the bishop, Ludovico's patron, blesses the voyage. Ludovico is flattered no less grossly in an elaborate device which occupies the lower half of the panel on the right. Here a well-grown and flourishing mulberry tree (Ital., *moro*), with white rabbits playing about its roots, stands within a wattled enclosure ; its trunk, the top of which is fashioned into a Moor's head, is embraced by a slender sapling symbolizing Gian Galeazzo, and on either side are scrolls bearing the legends, cruelly ironical when read by the light of events, " Gaude, fili, protector tuus ero semper " and " Dum vivis, tutus et letus vivo." In addition to the ducal arms, the border contains several Sforza emblems,

---

[1] It is fully described by Van Praet, *Livres Imprimés sur vélin*, 1822, v., p. 79, and d'Adda, *Indagini*, i., p. xxiii. ; and, for a facsimile, see Delaborde, *op. cit.*, p. 216. There is a third vellum copy in the Vatican, but the first page of the text, which no doubt had a border, has been cut out (Van Praet, p. 84).

such as the greyhound and tree, the brush, the well-known torches and fire-buckets, the dove with the motto " Merito et tempore," and the three plants of sempervivum with the motto " Mit zait "; and from the character of the decoration generally the volume was obviously a gift to Gian Galeazzo, either from Ludovico himself or from some one devoted to his interests. As might be expected, the border as a whole cannot vie in richness, beauty and taste with that in the Grenville Sforziada, which was Ludovico's own copy. The style, however, is so nearly analogous with that in the companion border that, if not actually by the same artist, it was probably executed under his direct inspiration.[1]

But, besides the printed Sforziada, the spoils of the Sforza library at Pavia, now in the Bibliothèque Nationale, also include a volume in manuscript which may claim the same title, although it deals with the exploits, not of Francesco Sforza, but of his father Muzio Sforza Attendolo.[2] The work itself was composed by Antonio Minuti of Piacenza in 1458, but the actual copy was written in 1491 by Bartolommeo Gambagnolo of Cremona to the order of Marchesino Stangha, ducal secretary, evidently for presentation to Ludovico. This MS. is more freely adorned than the two printed volumes, not only having two of its pages (ff. 1, 5) surrounded with elaborate borders, but a third page (f. 4 *b*) entirely given up to a pictorial design. Of the two borders, the first, though similar in style, ranks considerably below both those already noticed, its execution being coarser and the amorini and other figures in particular being comparatively weak. In many features, indeed, it recalls the less admirable specimens of Milanese work in the Book of Hours (above, p. xxii.). But, if this border, as seems most likely, was entrusted to a pupil, the second

---

[1] M. Delisle, the learned and courteous Director of the Bibliothèque Nationale, is of opinion that only the two portrait-busts are by the same hand.

[2] Bibl. Nat., MS. Ital. 372, " Compendio di gesti del magnanimo et gloriosissimo Signore Sforza," etc. It is described by Van Praet, *op. cit.*, v., p. 83, and by d'Adda, *Arch. Stor. Lomb.*, 1885, p. 772. See also Bradley, *Dict. of Miniaturists*, 1889, iii., p. 230.

approaches more nearly to the level of that in the Grenville Sforziada,[1] indications of a master-hand being again apparent; and, moreover, among other points of resemblance to the superior series of borders in Bona's MS., it shows the same deft adaptation of bunches of seed-pods and wheat-ears to decorative purposes which is there observable. There is a further reminiscence of the Grenville border in a boy Moor's head at the top of the page, and similarly also the central panel at the bottom displays the many-quartered shield of Ludovico's arms, which is supported in this case by only four amorini. However it may be with the page generally, neither these amorini nor a bust of Sforza Attendolo contained within the initial letter appear to be by the hand of the Grenville volume, agreeing more nearly in treatment with the full-page miniature opposite. This miniature represents an equestrian figure of Sforza Attendolo beneath a grand triumphal arch, and, although execution and colouring are not quite of the first order, the design is truly magnificent. The hand, however, is apparently distinct from any of those employed on the Book of Hours.

Including Bona's MS., we have thus four contemporary volumes connected with the Sforzas, two in MS. and two printed on vellum, the decoration of which, though evidently by more than one hand and of different degrees of excellence, presents essentially the same characteristics of style and even bears, so to speak, the imprint of the same studio. In addition, there is in the British Museum another note-worthy Milanese border, already alluded to (p. xxvii.), which belongs to the same class. This border is not in a volume, but on a separate sheet of vellum,[2] surrounding on three sides the upper half of a docu-ment which records a grant of lands by Ludovico il Moro to his wife,

---

[1] It is engraved, very unsatisfactorily, in Müntz, p. 47; where also, at p. 229, the miniature described below is reproduced.

[2] Add. MS. 21,413. It is in the hand of "Guspertus Cremonensis D. Pauli civis Mediolanensis," ducal chancellor and notary public, and bears Ludovico's signature. The upper portion of the border is engraved by Müntz, p. 233.

dated at Vigevano on 28th January, 1494, a few months before he became actual Duke of Milan. In the panel along the top are remarkably good medallion portraits of Ludovico[1] himself and Beatrice d'Este, and in the central compartment between them is a shield of their arms, surrounded by a wreath of foliage, flowers and fruit, and supported by two amorini ; while the side panels, the ground of which is mostly blue, are filled with renaissance designs, in which the brush, horse-bit, and other Sforza emblems and mottoes are conspicuous. With the large scale of the work,[2] the general effect is extremely fine ; but here also the peculiar distinction and charm that belong to the Grenville border and many in the Book of Hours are lacking, and the technique betrays a less facile exponent of the same style. According to the Marchese d'Adda, who is followed by Mr. Bradley,[3] the hand is identical with that of the MS. Sforziada at Paris. This, however, is on the very questionable assumption that in the latter volume a single artist was responsible for the whole of the work ; and, although in some of the details of the Vigevano document there are resemblances to one or other of the three pages above described, they are hardly conclusive as to actual identity of hand, being little more in fact than the common property of the school. The further opinion of the same authorities, attributing the decoration of both MSS. to the famous Franciscan miniaturist and illuminator Frà Antonio da Monza, is equally open to doubt ; for, good as the work is in both cases, it does not possess the masterly qualities of the signed miniature of the Descent of the Holy Spirit preserved in the Albertina Museum at Vienna.

[1] It may be remarked that none of the portraits of Ludovico here mentioned in the least bear out the statement of Giovio that his complexion was fair (Symonds, *Age of the Despots*, i., p. 483). He is said to have derived the name "Il Moro," not from his swarthiness, but from his emblem of a mulberry tree (*moro*); but the name, on the contrary, may have suggested the emblem, as in the case of the Moor's head.

[2] Along the top the border measures 21 inches by 4¼ inches, and the side panels are 14 inches long.

[3] *Arch. Stor. Lomb.*, 1885, p. 772 ; Bradley, *Dict. of Miniaturists*, iii., p. 242.

f

This splendid composition,[1] with the detached border within which it is
now laid down, is apparently all that survives of a MS. of grand pro-
portions illuminated by the artist for Pope Alexander VI. So far
as can be judged from a photograph, it has a nearer affinity to the
miniatures in Bona's Book of Hours (*e.g.* nos. 18 and 64) than to
that in the MS. Sforziada ; but neither miniature nor border is quite
similar in style to any of those here discussed, either in the Book of
Hours or elsewhere. Dr. Waagen, it should be mentioned, differs from
d'Adda as to Add. MS. 21,413, and, as it appears, for the worse ; but,
when he expressed the belief that it is a work of Girolamo da Milano,[2]
he was probably unacquainted with the very different style of that artist,
as displayed in the superb choral-books at Siena, illuminated by him
in conjunction with Liberale da Verona.

The attempt to assign an artist's name to the Grenville Sforziada
has not been more fortunate, though we find it spoken of with no less
confidence as "exhibiting a splendid specimen of the talents "[3] of Girolamo dai Libri, of Verona, equally well known as a miniaturist and as
a painter in oils on a larger scale. In 1490, when this border was
executed, Girolamo was only sixteen years old ; but the argument that
might therefore be drawn from the entire absence from it of any sign
of immature powers is weakened by the fact that a fine altar-piece at
Malcesine, on Lake Garda, was painted by him at exactly the same
early age.[4] There are, however, no valid grounds for connecting him
with so typical an example of Milanese work, and the idea probably
originated in little more than a guess. Subject to what will be said
lower down, this work indeed, like the rest, must for the present remain

---

[1] Engraved by Müntz, p. 195, and the border, p. 209. A photograph of both together
is in the *Arch. Stor. Lomb.*, 1885, p. 769. It is assumed that the border is by Frà Antonio,
but it came from a different part of the volume, or possibly from another MS. altogether.

[2] *Treasures of Art, Supplement*, 1857, p. 25. For G. da Milano see the *Arch. Stor.
Lomb.*, as above, p. 761, where d'Adda identifies him with G. da Cremona.

[3] H. Shaw, *Illuminated Ornaments*, 1833, no. xxxv.

[4] Kugler, 1887, i., p. 269 ; Crowe and Cavalcaselle, 1871, i., p. 494.

anonymous, and the main result of the comparison is that, whoever he was, the master who designed it was almost certainly employed also by the Duchess Bona on her Book of Hours, while less indubitable marks of his handiwork can be traced in the other two Sforziadas. At the same time, he was only one of several to whose co-operation Bona was indebted for a MS. which for the extent no less than the superlative excellence of its artistic embellishment is probably unique of its kind. Though it would be difficult to fix the precise lines of demarcation, the division of labour is most widely manifest in the borders, and it is questionable whether any of these are by the same hands as the full-page miniatures. In the latter, as we have seen (p. xii.), there are undoubtedly three distinct hands, and probably the number might be increased. A fourth, for example, appears to be represented by nos. 19–23 (above, p. xii.) in the series of the Passion, where not only are our Lord's features of a somewhat different type, but, notably in the scene before Caiaphas and in the " Ecce Homo," there is a display of violent action and coarse realism which seem out of harmony with Italian artistic sentiment and rather suggest that these miniatures, and possibly others, were the work of one of the German artists who are known to have studied at Milan. Otherwise the style throughout is plainly Milanese, or, more properly speaking, Lombard ; but unhappily the valuable researches of the Marchese d'Adda into the history of Milanese illumination were cut short by death, and his rough and disjointed notes for this special period, as printed in the *Archivio Storico Lombardo*, afford no more tangible clue than the letter of Giovanni Pietro Birago (p. viii.). Of this artist we know practically nothing, and the most that can be said is that he was certainly entrusted by the Duchess with the preparation of a costly service-book of the same kind, the whole of the work in which we are not obliged to conclude was to be by his own hand.

Quite recently, however, important evidence on the subject has been personally communicated by Dr. Müller-Walde, whose opinion derives weight from his long devotion to the study of Lionardo da Vinci and his

school.   In the painter of the majority of the miniatures he recognizes
the best of the artists whose hands appear in a copy of the Grammar of
Donatus in the Trivulziana Library at Milan.[1]   This MS. was mani-
festly designed for Massimiliano Sforza, eldest son of Ludovico il Moro,
and contains full-page portraits of both father and son, together with a
number of allegorical and other miniatures, in which, as well as in the
portrait just mentioned, Massimiliano is depicted as a boy of tender
years.   As he was born at the end of 1491 or early in 1492, and was
sent into Germany in September, 1499, before his father's final over-
throw, to be under the protection of the Emperor Maximilian, the
volume most probably dates from about 1498.   Judging from the
photographs obligingly lent by Dr. Müller-Walde for comparison, there
can be little doubt as to the identity of hand, though the examples in
the Book of Hours are more carefully finished.   The resemblance is
strongest in a miniature in which Massimiliano is seated before his
tutor intent on his studies, while five of his young companions are idly
engaged in various diversions in the same room.   Both in this scene
and in another a dwarf is introduced, as in plates iii. and ix. from Bona's
MS. ; and in a third, where the boy is standing between two female
figures typifying Virtue and Vice, the background contains rocks, trees
and buildings, with a river in the middle distance, precisely similar in
treatment to those in the latter volume.   But the chief point of interest
in Dr. Müller-Walde's communication lies in his strong belief that the
Donatus miniatures are the work of Ambrogio Preda or de Predis ;
for, if such be really the case, this artist, who has already been
mentioned as the painter of the Ambrosiana portrait of Bianca Maria
(p. xxiv.), must also have taken the leading part in decorating her
mother's Book of Hours.   Down to a recent period he seems to have
been entirely unknown, and the credit of being the first to call
attention to him belongs to Morelli.[2]   As regards the Donatus, this

---

[1] Cod. N. 2,167 ; see G. Porro, *Catologo dei Codici Manoscritti della Trivulziana*,
1884, p. 139.
[2] *Italian Masters in German Galleries*, transl. L. M. Richter, 1883, p. 413.

high authority is in agreement with Dr. Müller-Walde, including in his list of Preda's works [1] not only the two portraits of Ludovico and Massimiliano, but the miniatures also, though he makes some confusion between the Donatus MS. and the so-called "Libro del Jesus" in the same collection, which was also executed for Massimiliano and apparently by the same artists. [2] Preda's connection with the Sforza family began at least as early as 1482, when he is found described as "depintore" to Ludovico, and he was probably a relation, perhaps a son or younger brother, of "Christoforus de Predis," whose signature, with the date 1474, [3] is to be read on a fine miniature of Galeazzo Maria Sforza now at Turin. If, as has been plausibly suggested, [4] he was the artist who accompanied Bianca Maria to Innsbruck in 1493, and whom she styles in a letter "el nostro pinctore," he must have speedily returned home, for he was laid up at Milan with a kick from a horse in July, 1494; and the probability is that, like Ludovico's children, he took refuge with the Emperor when troubles fell upon Milan in 1499. Of two signed portraits among the works now attributed to him, one, of Francesco Archinto, was painted in 1494; the other, a profile of the Emperor Maximilian, who employed him in designing coins and tapestry as well as in painting, is dated 1502. It is a signal tribute to his merits as an artist that his pictures were at one time thought to be by Lionardo da Vinci, and latterly fresh interest has attached to his name from the discovery of his association with the latter in painting the altar-piece in the Church of San Francesco at Milan, of which the "Vierge aux Rochers" formed a part. Whether any of the borders in the Book of Hours, as well as the miniatures, should be tentatively

---

[1] See the account of the artist in his *Italian Painters*, transl. C. J. Ffoulkes, 1892, p. 180. Further particulars of him are given by E. Motta, "Ambrogio Preda e Leonardo da Vinci," in *Arch. Stor. Lomb.*, 1893, p. 972.

[2] Cod. N. 2,163; see Porro, p. 215.

[3] So Morelli, p. 188; but 1476 according to Motta, p. 986.

[4] Calvi, p. 47. While at Innsbruck he painted a portrait of Catherine, wife of the Archduke Sigismund. Is it possible that the Ambrosiana portrait, Morelli's identification of which with Bianca Maria is disputed, really represents this lady?

ascribed to him, it is difficult to say; but, although there is a lack of this class of work in the Donatus,[1] we are able to compare the two portraits there with those of Ludovico il Moro and his father in the border of the Grenville Sforziada, and the resemblance, more especially in the treatment of the eyes and the strongly marked curve of the nostrils, is such that it seems by no means improbable that this border and consequently others in the Book of Hours, if not in the other two Sforziadas, are by his hand.

Passing from the original portion of the MS. to its alien additions, dating, be it remembered, about thirty years later, the broad distinctions between the Italian and Flemish schools of miniature painting are at once apparent. Apart from their lovely backgrounds, the Flemish examples are as a rule simpler in motive and adhere more closely in their subjects to established types, while their more devotional feeling and softer tones of colour give them an air of repose which is lacking in their more brilliant rivals. At the same time, contiguity has not been without its effect, for Italian influence, though not always so strongly marked as in the Entry into Jerusalem (above, p. xiv.), is here and there observable both in a tendency to heighten the colouring and in some of the details, and it is quite clear that the later artists had the advantage of seeing the works of their predecessors. Unfortunately the Flemish miniatures generally have proved more difficult to reproduce with a satisfactory result than the others, and the attempt in more than one instance had to be abandoned; the six plates, however, actually given (lv.-lx.) fairly represent the whole series.

In the miniature of St. Mark (pl. lv.) the saint has a robe of soft lake, with a brown fur tippet and cuffs; his cloak is green, and his

---

[1] The only border is one in which there is no foliage or arabesque work. In each of the lateral panels is a youth, one holding a banner of the Sforza arms and the other a tall flaming cresset, with rising background covered with trees and buildings. At the top is a small medallion bust of Ludovico (much like the Grenville example), with a cornucopia on each side of it, and at the bottom are Ludovico's arms, between the torches and fire-buckets.

cap vermilion. The table is of dull gold, and is covered with a blue
cloth, which falls to the ground and serves the purpose of a carpet.
Both the seat and the writing-desk are also of gold, the latter having
a black sloping front; in the foreground the pavement is dark grey
with inlaid green and red disks; further back it is in a chequer-pattern
of bluish and reddish grey. The bases and capitals of the columns
are of gold, as are also the renaissance designs overlying the light-blue
shafts. The arcading is green bordered with gold, the vaulting dark
blue, and the walls pale violet; lastly, the curtains, together with the
canopy over the chandelier, are red. In the entablature in front, on a
dark lake ground, are the cryptic characters—" NRVAS : FИOARVIMI :
1519," which, if intended to conceal the name of the artist, have only
too effectually attained their object.[1] Among other miniatures which
seem to be by the same hand are the three reproduced in plates lvi.–
lviii., together with the rest of the series in nos. 7–14 (p. xii.). In
the Visitation (pl. lvi.) the Virgin is robed entirely in blue, her fair
hair being covered by a transparent white veil. St. Elizabeth has a
gown of pale lake shaded with blue, a long red cloak, and a blue hood
over a white coif. In the mountainous background, intersected by a
river, with trees on one bank and buildings on the other, there are
features of exceptional beauty. In pl. lvii., the Adoration of the Magi,
the Virgin is again in blue, with an under-garment of lake appearing
at the neck; the curtain behind her is a dark olive-green, and the
coverlet of her couch pale lake slightly touched with gold. On her
left stands Joseph, wearing a dark slate-coloured robe and holding in
his hand a bright red cap. The Magus kneeling on her right has a
richly brocaded cloak of lake and gold lined with ermine, showing the
sleeves and collar of a green garment beneath, and his purple cap
lined with brown fur is on the floor beside him. His features, it must
be confessed, have all the look of a portrait, and by analogy he should
represent the person for whom the miniature was painted. This,

---

[1] Possibly they are altogether meaningless, as it seems to have been a fashion among
miniaturists at this time to introduce a fanciful medley of letters in their work.

however, is hardly consistent with the part assigned above (p. xi.) to
Charles V. in the history of the MS., and it suggests the possibility
that, instead of being inherited and completed by the Emperor, the
volume was presented to him in its actual state by the individual who
is here portrayed.[1]   The negro Magus in the foreground is still more
splendidly clothed, having a tunic of white and gold, with a sleeveless
jacket of light bluish green ; his hose are bright red, his boots orange-
brown, and his cap purple.   The third Magus has a red tunic and a
blue cloak lined with grey fur, and holds in his hand a fur-lined purple
cap, while the two figures on his right are respectively in grey and
dark red.   The shafts of the columns are of red serpentine marble,
the bases, capitals, and entablature being all coloured a dark grey.
Exactly the same ruined building appears in the Adoration of the
Angels (no. 9), the columns, however, being on the other side.   This
miniature is a finely-coloured and impressive night-scene, in which the
Virgin and five angels, four kneeling and the other standing behind,
are adoring the infant Saviour, while Joseph appears in the doorway
holding a candle, and a sixth angel, with orange-coloured drapery and
wings, hovers lightly overhead.   In pl. lviii., the Presentation in the
Temple, the Virgin is clothed as in pl. lvii., Joseph in grey with a red
cloak, and Simeon in gold brocade over a white under-robe, his hood
being of soft grey with white edging.   The woman in front has a dress
of pale bluish green with long pendent sleeves, over which is a trailing
red gown, slightly touched with gold, having a yellow fringe round the
short sleeves and skirt ; the upper stage of her head-dress is crimson
and the lower stage blue, over a network of gold.   The columns are
of green and red serpentine, the bases of gold, the capitals of gold
and light blue, the architrave of gold, and the frieze of lake with gold

---

[1] Thus, in the beautiful "Isabella Book" (Add. MS. 18,851) in the British Museum,
which was given to Isabella of Castile, Charles's grandmother, by Francisco de Roias in
1497, the donor is depicted in the same scene and posture.   Add. MS. 18,852, another
fine Flemish MS., was executed for Charles's mother, the Infanta Joanna, wife of the
Archduke Philip.

scroll-work. On the right is a canopy of pale bluish green with gold tassels, and round the edge of it is another fanciful inscription— "OMRVN · HSИOF · EИAVN."

In the beautiful miniature illustrating "O Intemerata" (pl. lix.) the Virgin, who is draped as usual in blue, sits on a low balustrade of a dark grey colour, over which is spread a rich Turkey-pattern carpet, extending under her feet. The curtain behind her is of white and gold brocade, and the high back of the seat is decorated with a renaissance design in gold on a crimson ground, the outer border being of grey and the arched top formed of bands of gold, lake, green, crimson and blue. The four angelic musicians (one of whom, it will be noted, is playing an organ, while another blows the bellows) have robes of pale tints of lake and blue, with under-sleeves of green, lake and orange ; their wings being of somewhat darker tints of blue and red. The graceful design and soft and harmonious colouring of this miniature, together with the fine background, make it one of the special gems of the MS. There are indications in it of a different hand, and they appear still more strongly in the equally beautiful " Salve, Regina " (no. 15), which baffled the photographer. Here the Virgin is standing on a bank of clouds, the feet of the infant Saviour resting on her left hand and wrist, while His arms are round her neck ; she is clothed in a long white robe, most delicately patterned and stippled in gold, and bears a richly jewelled crown on her head. Her face is of the broad flat type with high forehead characteristic of the Flemish school, and her long fair hair floats over her shoulders. Behind her stretches an innumerable crowd of angelic choristers. These are all draped in blue, and the same colour pervades the whole of the background except at the four corners, at each of which is a cherub, with rainbow-tinted wings, amid clouds of orange-red tipped with gold.

But the finest, as well as the least conventional, of all the Flemish miniatures is the Martyrdom of St. Andrew (pl. lx.). The figure in front on the right wears a tunic of very pale gold and a looser upper-garment of light blue, with gold embroidery at the edge ; his hose are

g

black, his boots yellow, and his cap light grey, edged with gold. The scabbard of his sword is grey, the hilt crimson and gold, and in his left hand he bears a golden sceptre. Behind him to the right is a man clad in a long red robe with collar and cuffs of grey fur, and wearing a turban of pale yellow shaded with red. The soldier with the lance wears a black jacket with sleeves slashed with white, short grey slashed breeches, and boots of the same colour; his hat is red, with ostrich plumes of pale lake, orange and white. The executioner in the foreground has an orange-brown jerkin over a pale lake tunic, light slate-blue hose, and reddish-brown boots. His comrade wears a red tunic cut into strips at the shoulders and waist, and showing sleeves beneath of vivid green; his ragged breeches are slate-colour, his boots black, and his cap brown. The figure behind him is in a blue robe, having a crimson collar with gold bordering, and over his left shoulder he carries a cloak of pale lake heightened with gold. In the distance the green of the herbage and trees merges into exquisitely graduated shades of blue, while in an opening of the sky on a gold ground, exactly as in several of the Italian miniatures, appears a half-length figure of our Lord. Altogether, for firmness of hand, dramatic power and fine colouring, this page seems to stand by itself, and there is additional evidence of its being by another artist in the fact that the writing on the other side is different from that on any of the other leaves containing the Flemish miniatures.

Of the miniatures in the Flemish series of which no facsimile is here given, two have already been described, and a few words may be added about some of the others. No. 5, for example, which depicts the Nailing of Christ to the Cross, differs from all the rest in occupying only two-thirds of the page. Above it are three lines of text written on a scroll, at either end of which is a naked putto, busied in wrapping it round his body. In these putti, as well as in some conventional foliage on the surrounding green background, the Italian element is unmistakable, while, at the same time, among the spectators in the scene below is a decidedly Spanish-looking figure mounted on a mule. From the rather peculiar gold hatching on some of the drapery, and for other reasons, this page appears to have been painted by the same hand as the Entry into Jerusalem (no. 16), and the Raising of Lazarus (no. 63). In the latter there is a fine church in the background, and a more than ordinarily marked distinction has been made in the costumes of the two sisters, one being in cloth of gold with an elaborate head-dress and the other in a plain dull blue gown with a white apron and cap, like a serving-maid. The only other miniature that need be touched upon is that of David in Penitence (no. 55), which may be assigned, though not without doubt, to the same artist as that of St. Mark. The principal figure is strangely contorted and unnatural, but in the rest of the composition there is abundant merit. David is kneeling under an arched portico, the vaulting of which is closely copied from the Italian miniature of St. Matthew (no. 3), while the destroying angel, with three darts, appears in the sky overhead (1 Chron. xxi.). Facing the portico, with an intervening garden-plot, is a large open square, on the further side of which a king, no doubt meant for David himself, sits enthroned in a balcony, reviewing a crowd of people who pass in single file before him. In this scene, in which it is not difficult to detect a covert warning to the new emperor Charles V. not to indulge in inordinate pride, the architectural features, both in the square itself and down a street leading out of it, are of singular interest, and if they could be recognized they might solve the question where these Flemish miniatures were executed, just as the inscription in pl. lv., assuming it to have a meaning, might reveal to us the artist's name.

G. F. W.

I.

APPROPINQVABAT

III.

IV.

VI.

OBSECRO.

DEVS QVI

VIII.

OMNIPOENS

IX.

XI.

FAC NOS

XIII.

XIV.

XVII.

INTERCESIO

XVIII.

· PRESTA ·

DEVS QVI

XXIII.

XXIV.

ad loca penaru. ant.
Adoramus te rpe ꝫ
bñdicim̄ tibi. qa per
scam̄ crucē tuam re
demisti mundum. ꝟ.
Dñe exaudi. ꝛ. Et
clamor. Oratio :~
Omine iesu
rpe fili dei ꝫ
uiui pone pa
sionem crucē ꝫ mor

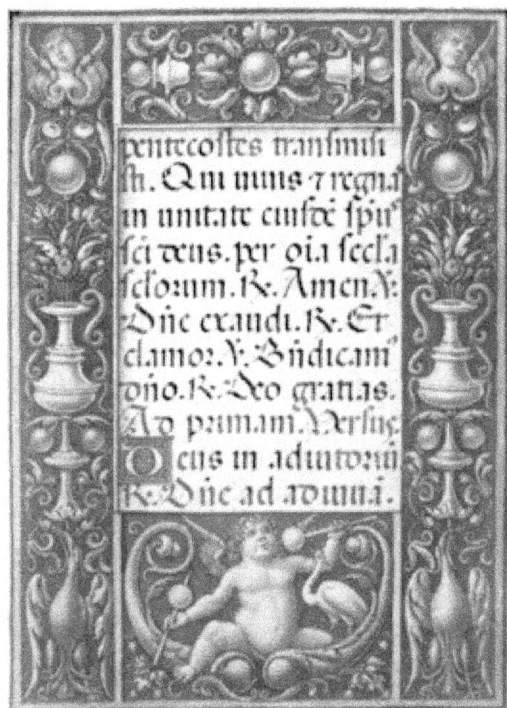

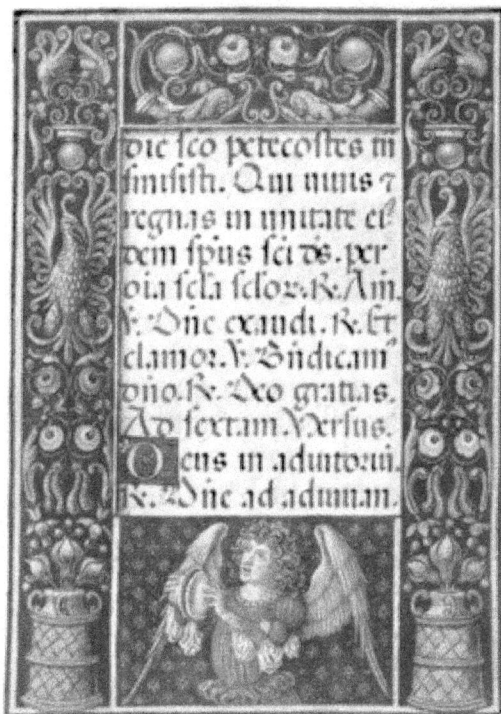

XXXII.

Omnipotens
sempiterne a
deus da nob
illam sancti spiritus
gratiam quam tuis
discipulis in die san
cto pentecostes trans
misisti. Qui vivis et
regnas in unitate ei
dem spiritus sancti
deus. per omnia sela

XXXVII.

XXXVIII.

trocinio confidentes.
perpetua defensione
conserua. Oratio.
OMnes sancti
tui quesumus
dne nos ubi
q3 adiuuent.ut dns
eorum merita recoli
mus patrocinia sen
tiamus. Et pacé tu
am nostris concedt

XLI.

XLIX.

cordenis peccata mea
dñe. Dum neneris in
dicare seculū p igne.
V. Dirige dñe deus
meus in ospectu tuo
uiam mea. Dum. In
terno nocturno. añ
Complaceat. ps. ds.
Xpectans ex
pectaui dñm
et intendit i

LI

Antare dño
canticum no
uum: laus ei
in ecclesia sanctoruz.
Letetur ifrael in eo
qui fecit eu: 7 filie si
on exultent in rege
suo. Laudent nom
eius in choro in tim
pano: 7 psalterio psal
lant ei Quia bnpla

LIV.

SEPTEM PSALMI
PENITENTIALES
INCIPIVNT ANT

Ne reminiscaris:
Omine ne i
furore tuo ar
guas me. ne
qz in ira tua corripi
as me. Miserere mei
domine quoniam in

DEVS. IN

LVII.

DEAS T ADVTORIV MEVM I TENDE.

O INTEMERATA·

CONCEDE NOBIS

LIBRO PRIMO DELLA HISTORIA DELLE COSE FACTE DALLO
INVICTISSIMO DVCA FRANCESCO SFORZA SCRIPTA IN LA
TINO DA GIOVANNI SIMONETTA ET TRADOCTA IN LIN
GVA FIORENTINA DA CHRISTOPHORO LANDINO FIOREN
TINO.

FRANCISCVS VIC.

PATER PATRIAE

NE TEMPI CHE LA REGINA GIOVANNA SE
conda figliuola di Carlo Re regnaua: perche era suc
ceduta nel regno Neapolitano a Larislao Re suo fra
tello: el quale parti di uita sanza figliuoli; Alphonso
Re daragona con grande armata mouendo di Cata
logna uenne in Sicilia ; Isola di suo Imperio. La cui
uenuta eccito gli huomini del Neapolitano regno a
quanti fauoriui a diuersi consigli: & non con piccoli
mouimenti di quel regno: Impero che Giouana Regina per molti & uarii
suoi impudichi amori era caduta in soma infamia. Et desperandosi che le:
femina potessi adempiere lofficio del Re: & administrare tanto regno; fece
a se marito Iacopo di Nerbona Conte di Marcia: el quale per nobilita di san
gue & belleza di corpo: ne meno per uirtu era tra Principi di Francia eccel
lente . Ma accorgendosi in breue che quello desiderata piu essere Re: che
marito: & quella non molto stimaua: mosso da seminile leuita lo rifiuto &
priuo dogni administratione . Questo fu cagione che'l suo regno: el quale per
sua natura e prono alle dissensioni & discordie: arrogendouisi e no honesti
costumi della Regina: ritorno nelle antiche fa ctioni & partialita: & comin
cio ogni giorno piu a fluctuare & uacillare. Erano alcuni a quali no dispia
ceua la signoria della dona: perche benche il nome fussi in lei loro; nientedi
meno comidauono. Altri desiderauano che Lodouico tertio Duca dangio:
figliuolo di Lodouico : e quale era nomato Re di Puglia; & di uol antenata:
della Reale stirpe daragonia: fussi adoptato dalla Regina. Costui poco auati
pe conforti di Martino tertio somo Pontefice: & di Sforza Attendolo excel
lentissimo Duca in militare disciplina : & padre di Francesco Sforza de cui
egregii facti habbiamo a scriuere: era uenuto a liti di Campagna: Et congiun
tosi Sforza: haueua mosso guerra alla Regina . Ma quegli che repugnauano
a Lodouico: metteuano ogni industria : che Alphonso fussi adoptato in fi
gliuolo della Reina: accio che in Napoli fussi tal Re: che con le sue forze &
di mare & di terra potessi resistere alla possa dg Francosi . Adunque in cosi
uehemente contentione de baroni: & piu huomini del regno: Alphonso chia
mato dalla Reina in herede & compagno del regno: d' uno no solo illustre:
ma anchora horribile : Et el nome Catelano el quale infino a quegli tempi
no era molto noto & celebre se non a popoli maritimi: ma inuerso & odioso:
comincio a crescere : & farsi chiaro . Ma & da Lodouico & da Sforza tanto
ogni giorno piu erano oppressi: el Re & la Regina: che diffidadosi nelle pro
prie forze: conduxono Braccio Perugino : el quale era el secondo Capitano:
di militia in Italia in quegli tépi cō molte honoreuoli códitioni: & maxime

LXII

LIBRO PRIMO DELLA HISTORIA DELLE COSE FACTE DALLO
INVICTISSIMO DVCA FRANCESCO SFORZA SCRIPTA IN LA
TINO DA GIOVANNI SIMONETTA ET TRADOCTA IN LIN
GVA FIORENTINA DA CHRISTOPHORO LANDINO FIOREN
TINO.

FRAN·SFOR·VIC
DVX
MII IIII
PATER PATRIAE

N E TEMPI CHE LA REGINA GIOVANNA SE
conda figliuola di Carlo Re regnaua:perche era suc
ceduta nel regno Neapolitano a Latislao Re suo fra
tello:elqual parti di uita sanza figliuoli:Alphonso
Re daragona con grande armata mouendo di Cata
logna uenne in Sicilia ; Isola di suo Imperio. La cui
uenuta excito gli huomini del Neapolitano regno a
uarii fauori:& a diuersi consigli:& non con piccoli
mouimenti di quel regno:Impero che Giouana Regina per molti & uarii
suoi impudichi amori era caduta in soma infamia.Et desperandosi che lei

LXIII.

www.ingramcontent.com/pod-product-compliance
Lightning Source LLC
Chambersburg PA
CBHW020542270326
41927CB00006B/692